THE ATONEMENT

Covered by the Blood

Rod Parsley

Columbus, Ohio

The Atonement: Covered by the Blood

ISBN: 1935794124
Copyright © 2014 by Rod Parsley

Published by:

Results Publishing
P.O. Box 100
Columbus, Ohio 43216-0100 USA

All Scripture quotations are taken from the *King James Version* of the Bible.

CONTENTS

Chapter One

Seven Celebrations in Three Seasons

No novelist would have dared to come up with such a story line, and no film director would have ever had the courage to pitch the concept to a studio: a collection of ragtag slaves, living in forced labor for generations, rises up under the influence of a charismatic leader, shakes off the shackles of bondage, overthrows the military might of the greatest empire on earth and makes their way to a homeland that is flowing with milk and honey.

This tale is not the fictional account of some fantastic culture in a faraway galaxy. It is the biblical story of the children of Israel leaving the slavery of Egypt for the sufficiency of the Promised Land under the direction of God and the guidance of Moses.

But the way to their promised possession was not a direct route. First, they made what must have seemed like a detour through the wilderness to Mount Sinai, where God gave them a set of laws which He expected them to obey so that they could live and prosper to fulfill His purpose.

While they were there, God gave them instructions about everything from how to properly worship Him to what to eat. Included in these instructions were specific commands about special convocations to be held at certain times of the year, to keep God and His word in proper perspective in their personal and national consciousness. These convocations were so important that they are covered thoroughly not once or twice, but three times in the Bible—in Exodus 23, Numbers 28-29 and Deuteronomy 16.

Leviticus 23:1-2 say:

And the LORD spake unto Moses, saying, Speak unto the children of Israel, and say unto them, Concerning the feasts of the LORD, which ye shall proclaim to be holy convocations, even these are my feasts.

The word feast as used here doesn't mean a holiday meal, such as our Thanksgiving. It is an appointed or fixed time, season or cycle to assemble and to celebrate. In addition, God said of them that they were His feasts—not Israel's feasts.

Our God is a God of seasons, cycles, timing and purpose. Time does not restrict Him or limit Him in any way as it does us, but

THE ATONEMENT

He always does things in their proper season to fulfill a particular purpose. He instructed the children of Israel to observe three seasons of celebration, involving seven different feasts. Each of these celebrations had a purpose, and each of them had prophetic impact as well.

The first of these feasts to be commemorated was Passover, held in the spring. It was instituted by God in Exodus 12 as a means for a nation in bondage to remember the great deliverance God gave them in bringing them out of slavery in Egypt. The Passover season also included two other feasts: Unleavened Bread and Firstfruits.

Passover is a powerful story. I'll talk about its prophetic significance later, but let me give you a brief overview. The households of Israel were commanded to kill a lamb in the evening on the fourteenth day of the first month. They were to take the blood and place it on the doorposts and the lintel of their house. By doing so, they would give evidence of their faith in God, and death would not touch them. Then they were to roast the lamb and eat it, without breaking any bones and making sure to finish it all. They were also supposed to eat it with unleavened bread and bitter herbs. Finally, they were to partake of the lamb while fully dressed and ready to travel—since the Lord had already arranged for their departure.

During their meeting with God at Sinai, Israel received instructions about two additional feasts that were included during the Passover season—Unleavened Bread and Firstfruits.

The feast of Unleavened Bread began immediately after Passover, and was a seven-day period when none of the households in

Israel could use or even possess leaven—a type of sin. Then, the day after the feast of Unleavened Bread began was another feast called Firstfruits, where the first sheaf of the barley harvest was waved before the Lord by the high priest as thanks for the harvest of the year.

These three feasts comprised the first feast season, together known as Passover.

The next feast was one that stood on its own in the summer, and marked the start of the wheat harvest. It was seven sabbaths following the feast of Firstfruits, and was called the feast of Weeks, and also became known as Pentecost, since it was fifty days after the Passover season.

The third season of feasts was in the fall, and also consisted of three separate feasts that were held in close proximity to one another. This season included the feast of

Trumpets, the Day of Atonement and the feast of Tabernacles. The feast of Trumpets was one day that involved blowing trumpets to announce a solemn assembly and a time of repentance. The Day of Atonement was the most important day of the year, since it was on this day that the high priest went into the Holy of Holies to offer sacrifices for all of Israel before the presence of God. The feast of Tabernacles lasted for seven days, when the families of Israel were commanded to dwell in booths, or temporary dwellings, symbolizing their acknowledgement of God's presence during their wilderness wanderings, and their thankfulness for permanent homes in the Promised Land. It was followed by a special sabbath on the eighth day.

All three of these fall feasts surrounded the ingathering of the fruits of the land, such as olives, grapes, dates and other produce. The three of them taken together were called the feast of Tabernacles.

The prophetic significance of all of these feasts is undeniable, but I want to focus especially on the season of fall feasts, collectively called Tabernacles. We'll examine them more carefully next.

Chapter Two

The Season of Tabernacles

Sometimes during a discussion of the cycles of God's feasts, people will ask why there wasn't a feast for the winter season. Even though many Jews the world over do observe Hanukkah, it is not included in the feasts God spoke to Moses about in the Pentateuch. It was added during the period of time between the close of the Old Testament and the beginning of the New Testament, when the Maccabees cleansed the Temple after it was polluted by a Syrian emperor.

The feasts under consideration here are those designated by God Himself. Since travel was required and was more difficult in winter, it stands to reason that God would not require His people to go to the expense and inconvenience of making their way to

Jerusalem during a time of cold and rain. And even though winters in Israel are more temperate than many other places in the world, I have seen snow on the mountains there—and not just Mount Hermon in the north, which is snowcapped for much of the year.

As I have already mentioned, the feasts of the Lord total seven in all, falling into three specific seasons—Passover in the spring, Pentecost in the summer and Tabernacles in the fall. Passover has already been memorialized by God, since that was the time of the crucifixion and resurrection of Christ by the power of God. In addition, Pentecost was also memorialized by the outpouring of the Holy Ghost, as we see in Acts 2. The only one of these three feast seasons that has not been memorialized by something significant that God does is

Tabernacles, and that is where I want to focus our attention.

Moving through the summer season into the fall presents a number of obstacles for people in every walk of life. In our culture, the latter half of summer is a time for families to finish their vacations and prepare for their children to go back to school. Other activities are often curtailed. The hottest days of summer for those living in the northern hemisphere usually happen at this time. People feel drained of initiative and energy. Economic activity slows down. Church attendance suffers. Uneasiness and irritability are heightened due to the heat and humidity. Stale, stagnant air stays in urban areas for days on end.

The ancients called this period of time the dog days of summer. They named it that because it corresponded with the rising of the most brilliant star in the night sky, Sirius, which was easily seen in the heavens just before sunrise during late summer. Sirius is the most easily identifiable star in the constellation Canis Major, or the large dog, found near the constellation Orion, the hunter. Since Sirius was the most notable star in the dog constellation, it became known as the Dog Star. They believed that its brightness, even though it could not be seen during the day, added to the heat of the sun, causing the highest temperatures of the year. They had no way of knowing that the extreme distances in the heavens prohibited even the brightest of stars from affecting earth's temperature (other than the sun, of course).

I think it is notable that some of the most horrific events in recent history have occurred during this period of time leading up to the season of Tabernacles. Many of the wars in history have begun during this period.

World War II began with Germany's invasion of Poland on September 1, 1939. In addition, the persecution of Jews reached new levels of severity during the same month. Japan made the decision to bomb Pearl Harbor in September of 1941.

In 1973, Israel's enemies decided to attack on Yom Kippur, the Day of Atonement. Even though they were vastly outnumbered in both men and machinery, Israel beat back Egyptian and Syrian advances and even went on the offensive on both fronts in nineteen days of fighting.

We will never forget the tragic events of September 11, 2001, ("9/11") when nearly 3,000 people lost their lives as a result of four aircraft being hijacked and used as flying bombs. Three of the aircraft crashed into buildings and one crashed on the ground.

THE ATONEMENT

On September 11, 2012, the U.S. Consulate in Benghazi, Libya was attacked, resulting in the death of four Americans, including Ambassador Christopher Stevens.

Besides all these events, more natural disasters occur during this season of the year than any other, including earthquakes, volcanic eruptions and hurricanes.

There is a reason for all this. Satan knows that the most important season of the year is the time of Tabernacles. He has not been able to stop any of the pieces of God's grand design for human history from continuing, but that does not keep him from attempting to thwart God's purpose. He is doomed to fail, but God's purposes will prevail—as they ultimately do.

Could it be that the reason Satan is so determined to cause problems on the earth during this season of the year is because he is aware of something that we have missed? This third great season in God's timetable has not yet been memorialized, as Passover and Pentecost have. What is it that God has in mind for this season of the year? We can find clues in the directions God gave Moses regarding these three fall feasts.

The first of these was the feast of Trumpets. It was held on the first day of the seventh month, and derived its name from the sounding of trumpets on that day. These trumpets were originally two in number, each made of one piece of silver and used according to the instructions God gave Moses in Numbers 10:1-10. Jews call this this day Rosh Hashanah, or "the head of the year." This is because it is the beginning of a new year according to their calendar, which is quite different from the calendar used in the western world. Passover is regarded as the beginning of the Jewish religious year, but

THE ATONEMENT

Trumpets is the start of the new civil year, when the Jewish calendar increases the year number. Sabbath and Jubilee years begin at Trumpets, not at Passover.

There were four themes to the feast of Trumpets, according to Jewish tradition. First, according to the Talmud (the Jewish commentary on the Torah, or law), God created man on the first day of the month Tishri, so that is commemorated by the feast of Trumpets as the new year. This is logical, since the day of man's creation would be when the history of man began. Trumpets is also regarded as a day of judgment, which gives an opportunity for cleansing, repentance, to right past wrongs and to vow to do better in the coming year. Those who do so have their names written in the book of life, and their names are sealed ten days later on the Day of Atonement. The period between the feast of Trumpets and the Day of

Atonement is known to Jews as the Days of Awe.

The feast of Trumpets is also a day of remembrance, since according to Jewish tradition, Abraham offered Isaac as a sacrifice on this day, and substituted a ram instead (see Genesis 22). Finally, the sound of the trumpets being blown during the feast of Trumpets has three meanings. First, it recalls the story of Abraham, Isaac and the ram offered as a sacrifice. But it also com- memorates a coronation. Trumpets were traditionally blown whenever a king ascended to the throne in Israel. On this day, God is acknowledged as king over all humanity, and especially recognized as king over His chosen people, the children of Israel. Third, trumpets being sounded on this feast day reminded Jews of God's omnipotence, His omni- presence and of their opportunity to partake of His mercy.

21

THE ATONEMENT

Ten days after the feast of Trumpets came the Day of Atonement. This was generally regarded as the most holy day of the year, since it was the one day every year when the high priest went into the presence of God in the Holy of Holies to make atonement for the sins of Israel—first in the Tabernacle and later in the Temple, according to Leviticus 16:30:

> *For on that day shall the priest make an atonement for you, to cleanse you, that ye may be clean from all your sins before the LORD.*

This day gave all repentant Jews the chance to begin the new year with their sins covered—they had the chance to start over again, trusting in God's mercy and grace so that they could live in a manner that was pleasing to Him.

The Season of Tabernacles

This was followed five days later by the beginning of the feast of Tabernacles, when Israel was commanded to build temporary structures, or booths, of tree branches to dwell in for seven days. This was to be a time of rejoicing, commemorating the time Israel spent in the presence of the Lord in the wilderness, and thanksgiving that He had brought them into their promised possession.

The Passover season has great prophetic impact. The lamb that Israel killed not only provided protection from death because of the blood applied to their households, it also meant physical healing for them as they prepared for their journey out of Egypt and into the land of their promise. That lamb was a type of the Lamb of God, Jesus Christ, whose blood was shed for the sins of the whole world on Calvary's cross. Jesus is also our Healer, providing physical healing for us through faith in His name.

The feast of Unleavened Bread is also prophetic, since it forecasts a time when God's people would be able to live free from the destructive force of sin, symbolized by leaven. This freedom is not as a result of our own effort, but because of the effective work of Christ on the cross, redeeming us from sin's power and enabling us to live free from its corrupting influence.

The feast of Firstfruits is prophetic as well, since the barley sheaf waved by the priest was symbolic of the first of the entire year's harvest. If that sheaf was accepted, the harvest was also accepted. Jesus appeared before the throne of God as our Firstfruits, and He was accepted, so all who believe in Him as Savior are also accepted as part of the great harvest of the earth.

Pentecost, too, has been memorialized by the great outpouring of the precious Holy Spirit, who was sent in overflowing measure as recorded in Acts chapter 2. The empowering and enabling of the Holy Ghost has been equipping men and women ever since that first century event. Now we are able to do what Jesus commanded us to do, which is go into all the world and preach the gospel to every creature (Mark 16:15).

The only one of these three feast seasons that has not yet been memorialized by a sovereign act of God is Tabernacles. I want to show you why—but first, I want to tell you what happened on the Day of Atonement.

Chapter 3

The Day of Atonement

The specific procedures to be followed on the Day of Atonement were announced by God to Moses in Leviticus 16. The work to be done that day focused on the high priest, who was to represent all Israel by taking an offering of blood into the presence of God in the Holy of Holies and sprinkling it on the mercy seat to make atonement for the sins of the nation. This is so important, and such a foreshadowing of the work of our great High Priest, Jesus Christ, that I want to deal with it in more detail.

According to Numbers 10:10, the trumpet was to be blown over the sacrifices that were made on every feast day. The Day of Atonement was a solemn assembly (the most celebrated of all of them throughout the year), so the trumpet would certainly have been blown on that day.

It's our responsibility to sound the alarm about the danger men are in as a result of sin. Lots of people don't want to talk about it, but it's just as true now as it ever was—according to Romans 6:23, "...*the wages of sin is death.*" Ezekiel 18:4 says, "...*the soul that sinneth, it shall die.*" James 1:15 declares: "...*sin, when it is finished, bringeth forth death.*"

Man found himself in danger of judgment from a righteous and holy God as a result of sin. But thank God, He did not leave us in this deplorable condition—lost and separated from all that is righteous and holy because of sin. God provided a substitute—a holy and spotless Lamb who would provide a sinless sacrifice that paid the price demanded by sin to redeem every soul and pay the ransom that was required, so that once again sinful man could be reconciled to a holy God.

This act of reconciliation was foreshadowed by the activity that took place on the Day of Atonement. It occurred once every year, just as Jesus went to the cross one time for the sins of the whole world. It happened at an appointed season—a due time, according to Romans 5:6: *"For when we were yet without strength, in due time Christ died for the ungodly."* There are four things I want to point out about the Day of Atonement.

First, we see the person of this great day—the high priest. As he fulfills his God-given duties on the Day of Atonement, we see him as a figure of our High Priest, Jesus Christ. Let's look more closely at this man and what he did on the day our sins were covered by the blood of an innocent sacrifice.

THE ATONEMENT

The high priest was stripped—that is, he did not wear his usual garments of purple and blue and gold. He took off all those vestments and wore only a simple robe of white linen on the day when he went into the presence of God. He did not appear before God in all of his priestly finery—he was there as a humble worshipper, representing people who came not claiming great rights, but beseeching great mercies.

When Jesus was offered as a sacrifice, He did not come into God's presence in glory, but in humility. He was stripped of all dignity and was completely exposed to the brutality of the Roman guards and the contempt of passersby. His only crown was cruel thorns; his robe was taken from him and became the prize of soldiers playing a game of chance.

The high priest was spotless. He had to undergo multiple cleansings and was required to offer a blood sacrifice for himself before he was able to represent anyone else. Incense went before him as he entered into the presence of God.

Our High Priest, too, was spotless—a Lamb born without sin, so that He would be able to satisfy the demands of justice and the law. One sinless life was taken in a garden in Genesis 3; another sinless life must be offered to make the necessary atonement. Only pure blood, untainted by sin that infected all of Adam's race, would provide the antidote for the contagion that brought death to all who contracted it. Hebrews 4:15 says:

> *For we have not an high priest which cannot be touched with the feeling of our infirmities; but was in all points tempted like as we are, yet without sin.*

THE ATONEMENT

Second Corinthians 5:21 says:

For he hath made him to be sin for us, who knew no sin; that we might be made the righteousness of God in him.

The high priest was solitary. He had to go alone into the Holy of Holies. No other human being was allowed to accompany him or help him. He had to part the veil and appear in the presence of the Almighty God without aid of any sort. The future of the entire nation rested upon his shoulders. Whether or not sin was covered for another year would depend solely upon the proper fulfillment of his office. One error would mean disaster for not only himself and his family, but for all who relied upon his faithful service.

Jesus also did His work of redemption alone. Beginning in the garden of

Gethsemane, He labored under the light of a full Passover moon while even the closest of His companions slept in ignorance of the awful burden He carried. He alone was tied to the whipping post, surrounded by Roman soldiers who were calculating and exacting in their work with the scourge. He was alone among the multitudes as they prodded Him through the cobblestone streets of Jerusalem. And even though He was crucified between thieves and surrounded by mockers, He was alone before God as He carried out His work of offering an atoning sacrifice for the sins of not just one nation, but of all humanity.

The high priest's duties were strenuous. He had fifteen beasts to slaughter, skin and cut into sections to fulfill the divine prescription for the Day of Atonement; and he had to wash himself at least five times during the day. He had to take the blood and sprinkle it on the mercy seat. It was activity that required strength that was beyond ordinary.

Jesus Christ also required extraordinary strength as He contemplated carrying a burden beyond any that had ever been assigned to the sons of men. The physical trauma alone would have been enough to either kill lesser men or at least render them unconscious. He was betrayed by one of His own and abandoned by the others. He was falsely accused and questioned repeatedly without the benefit of food or rest. He was scourged without mercy and crucified without pity. But beyond all that, He carried with Him the burden of every sin and iniquity that had ever been named among men. No wonder He stumbled on His way to Golgotha.

In addition to the person of the Day of Atonement, we also see the procedure that was used. The day centered on a sacrifice—

actually, many sacrifices—that were prescribed to insure that all of Israel would be
covered by the blood that was sprinkled
before the presence of God in the Holy of
Holies. The picture of a sinless substitute
offered in place of the guilty was repeated
over and over again for all those assembled.

The blood of those offerings on the
Day of Atonement painted a crimson portrait
of another sinless sacrifice who would
willingly offer Himself on the cross: the
Lamb of God—the ultimate Lamb to which
all other sacrifices pointed for fulfillment.

In addition, the Day of Atonement had
another important feature, called the
scapegoat. This process, outlined in Leviticus
16, involved casting lots over two goats. One
would be sacrificed as a sin offering, and the
other would be released in the wilderness
after the high priest laid his hands on its head

and confessed the sins of the nation over it. This symbolized that the sins of the people would be removed from them, never to be dealt with again.

Not only is Jesus our High Priest, He was also our scapegoat. He took the sins of the world upon Himself and bore them away so that we would never have to deal with them again. As a result of His sacrifice, we can live free from sin and the fear of judgment.

The product of the Day of Atonement was very simple: what was unacceptable and unholy was made acceptable and holy. Iniquity and unrighteousness were covered by the blood of atonement applied to the mercy seat in the presence of God. The veil was penetrated by the blood of a sinless sacrifice, used to cover the faults and failings of fallen man. Freedom to all who trusted in that sacrifice was announced with joy as the high priest came out of the Holy of Holies after making the prescribed offering. Every fiftieth year was a year of Jubilee, when debts were released, slaves were set free and every man, regardless of what condition he was in, was allowed to return to his rightful possession to enjoy all the benefits of his birthright.

Because of what Jesus, our High Priest, has done, we can walk free from the condemnation that sin brings and enjoy our inheritance as the people of God. He not only covered our sin with His blood, He took it away as though it never existed. Through faith in His shed blood, we now have access to the throne of God, not just on one special day a year, but at any time.

The cross was the price of access into God's holy presence. Our unrighteousness has been exchanged for His righteousness; our death for His life; our sorrow for His joy; our poverty for His abundance. The trumpet of Jubilee has been blown, and we are no longer estranged by sin from what God has always intended for us to possess. Now all that He has planned has been purchased; we can walk in the newness and abundance that has been purchased for us by His great sacrifice.

Finally, there is the perfection of the Day of Atonement. This is something that was prefigured by the events of the day in ancient Israel, but is only fully demonstrated to us as believers. The work of the high priest in Leviticus 16 has been fully and finally completed by our High Priest, Jesus Christ. Other than the high priest, there was no work allowed to be done by anyone else on that day. So it is today. We cannot achieve by religious works what has already been accomplished and must be received by faith.

We must accept as generous gifts what God has done and wants us to enjoy by His grace.

Let me illustrate this by an acronym that will help you identify the blessings of the grace of God.

G-R-Λ-C-E is the perfection that results from the Day of Atonement. *G* stands for gift, which is the principle of grace. It cannot be earned; it must be received. *R* stands for redemption, which is the purpose of grace. Without God's grace, redemption would never have been achieved nor offered to humanity. *A* stands for access, which is the privilege of grace. Now those who were once denied are welcomed into the presence of God. *C* stands for character, which is the product of grace. When we come into God's presence, we are transformed to become more like Him. Finally, *E* stands for eternal life, which is the prospect of grace. Once we have received it, we can live forever in His glorious presence.[1]

If that weren't enough, there are more blessings available to all who will access them. I want to tell you about them next.

---

[1] Vance Havner, *Truth for Each Day*, (Westwood, New Jersey, 1962), 27.

Chapter 4

Seven Blessings of the Atonement

Joel 2:21-32 say:

Fear not, O land; be glad and rejoice: for the LORD will do great things. Be not afraid, ye beasts of the field: for the pastures of the wilderness do spring, for the tree beareth her fruit, the fig tree and the vine do yield their strength.

Be glad then, ye children of Zion, and rejoice in the LORD your God: for he hath given you the former rain moderately, and he will cause to come down for you the rain, the former rain, and the latter rain in the first month. And the floors shall be full of wheat, and the fats shall overflow with wine and oil.

THE ATONEMENT

And I will restore to you the years that the locust hath eaten, the cankerworm, and the caterpillar, and the palmerworm, my great army which I sent among you. And ye shall eat in plenty, and be satisfied, and praise the name of the LORD your God, that hath dealt wondrously with you: and my people shall never be ashamed. And ye shall know that I am in the midst of Israel, and that I am the LORD your God, and none else: and my people shall never be ashamed.

And it shall come to pass afterward, that I will pour out my spirit upon all flesh; and your sons and your daughters shall prophesy, your old men shall dream dreams, your young men shall see visions: And also upon the servants and upon the handmaids in those days will I pour out my spirit.

And I will shew wonders in the heavens and in the earth, blood, and fire, and pillars of smoke. The sun shall be turned into darkness, and the moon into blood, before the great and the terrible day of the LORD come.

And it shall come to pass, that whosoever shall call on the name of the LORD shall be delivered: for in mount Zion and in Jerusalem shall be deliverance, as the LORD hath said, and in the remnant whom the LORD shall call.

You may wonder what a reference to Joel, traditionally known as the prophet of Pentecost, is doing in a book about the feast of Tabernacles, and especially the Day of Atonement. There can be no doubt that a portion of Joel's prophetic utterance recorded in this chapter was fulfilled on the day of

Pentecost, recorded in Acts chapter 2. Peter certainly understood it to be so, and quoted Joel when explaining what had happened to the multitudes who gathered together on that day, attracted by the sound of a rushing mighty wind (see Acts 2:16-21). But there is nothing wrong with recognizing that a prophetic utterance can have its fulfillment in more than one period of time. Peter himself said in Acts 2:39:

> *For the promise is unto you, and to your children, and to all that are afar off, even as many as the Lord our God shall call.*

Knowing more about the time surrounding the season of Tabernacles gives us additional understanding about Joel's prophecy. The prophet is undoubtedly talking about a time of restoration that precedes the Lord's returning. Joel 2:23 talks about the former rain and the latter rain falling in the first month. As we have seen, the feast of Trumpets marks the beginning of the year in the Jewish civil calendar. That means the time of Joel's prophesied end-time outpouring is coming during the season of Tabernacles.

Earlier in chapter 2, Joel calls for a time of repentance that comes before restoration. This coincides with the ten days of repentance that take place between the feast of Trumpets and the Day of Atonement. After that, God promises to pour out unparalleled blessing on His people. In fact, there are seven distinct blessings God outlined in Joel 2—seven blessings available on the Day of Atonement—and I want to point them out to you.

The first atonement blessing is a double portion. Joel 2:23 talks about the former rain and the latter rain coming at the same time. This indicates a double portion of blessing—more than enough, too much, overflow and double for your trouble!

The second atonement blessing is financial abundance, according to Joel 2:24: when the threshing floors will be full of wheat, the wine vats will overflow with new wine and the olive presses will yield an abundance of oil. When Israel was prosperous, these commodities were always present in abundant quantities. God wants to bless the work of your hands with an abundance of finances for every good work.

The third atonement blessing is restoration. Joel 2:25 speaks of God restoring everything that the locust in all of its forms has destroyed. Get ready to get back everything the devourer has stolen from you!

The fourth atonement blessing is miracles. Joel 2:26 says God will deal wondrously with you. Signs and wonders are part of your future. God is about to do such great things in your life that people will see it and have to say, "No man could have done this!"

The fifth atonement blessing is God's divine presence. Joel 2:27 declares that God will be in your midst in such a way that you will never be put to shame. When God speaks, others have to be quiet. When God shows up, anyone not in agreement with Him slinks back into the darkness.

The sixth atonement blessing is upon your family. Joel 2:28-31 talk about the marvelous way God will reveal Himself to everyone in your household—sons and daughters, young and old, servants and handmaidens. Nobody is left out as God moves supernaturally in these last days.

The seventh atonement blessing is deliverance. Joel 2:32 says that whosoever shall call upon the name of the Lord shall be saved. Salvation is not a term that just means forgiveness of sins and a ticket punched to go to heaven. Salvation is an all-inclusive term that means you are set free from whatever has you bound.

As I said before, Passover has been memorialized by the crucifixion and resurrection of Jesus Christ from the grave. Pentecost has been memorialized by the outpouring of the Holy Spirit. Tabernacles has not yet been memorialized—but I believe it will be—and soon.

Jesus made it clear that no man knew the day or the hour of His appearing (see Matthew 24:36). However, He also gave us signs of His coming, and told us to be watchful (see Matthew 24:32-33).

First Thessalonians 4:16-17 say:

For the Lord himself shall descend from heaven with a shout, with the voice of the archangel, and with the trump of God: and the dead in Christ shall rise first: Then we which are alive and remain shall be caught up together with them in the clouds, to meet the Lord in the air: and so shall we ever be with the Lord.

Could it be that the feast of Trumpets, which begins the new year for the Jews, will be commemorated by the appearing of Jesus Christ in the clouds to receive His own in an event known as the rapture? Is it possible that the trumpets blown to commemorate the start of the fall feast season are only prophetic forecasts of God's trumpet, which will sound out from heaven to awaken those who have gone before us, having died in faith?

THE ATONEMENT

This hope that we have from the Lord is not just an escape mechanism to get us out of terrible conditions on the earth. On the contrary, God intends it to be the exclamation point of exemplary lives that are witnesses of the grace and glory of an omnipotent God. When the time is right, He simply comes and receives those saints who are alive on the earth to Himself to join all the rest who are already gathered together in heaven.

I should mention one more thing—the bodies of those who have died will be resurrected from the grave into bodies that are immortal and will be able to withstand the glories of heaven. Those who are alive will be changed in a moment, according to 1 Corinthians 15:51-54.

You may be asking the question, "What if He doesn't come this year during this season? What happens then?"

According to the prophet Joel, if the Lord doesn't return during the season of Tabernacles, we get a double portion of blessing. We win, the devil loses. Either way, I'm going to rejoice!

Addendum

Read the following Scriptures to help you have a greater understanding of the importance of the seven feasts. (The passages in Numbers 28 and 29 are not included here, since they only deal with the kinds and amounts of sacrifices that were required for each of the feasts.)

> *Three times thou shalt keep a feast unto me in the year. Thou shalt keep the feast of unleavened bread: (thou shalt eat unleavened bread seven days, as I commanded thee, in the time appointed of the month Abib; for in it thou camest out from Egypt: and none shall appear before me empty:) And the feast of harvest, the firstfruits of thy labours, which thou hast sown in the field: and the feast of*

ingathering, which is in the end of the year, when thou hast gathered in thy labours out of the field. Three times in the year all thy males shall appear before the Lord GOD.

~Exodus 23:14-16

And the LORD spake unto Moses after the death of the two sons of Aaron, when they offered before the LORD, and died; And the LORD said unto Moses, Speak unto Aaron thy brother, that he come not at all times into the holy place within the vail before the mercy seat, which is upon the ark; that he die not: for I will appear in the cloud upon the mercy seat. Thus shall Aaron come into the holy place: with a young bullock for a sin offering, and a ram for a burnt offering. He shall put on the holy linen coat, and he shall have the linen breeches upon his flesh, and shall be girded with a linen girdle, and with the linen mitre shall he be attired: these are holy garments; therefore shall he wash his flesh in water, and so put them on.

And he shall take of the congregation of the children of Israel two kids of the goats for a sin offering, and one ram for a burnt offering. And Aaron shall offer his bullock of the sin offering, which is for himself, and make an atonement for himself, and for his house. And he shall take the two goats, and present them before the LORD at the door of the tabernacle of the congregation.

THE ATONEMENT

And Aaron shall cast lots upon the two goats; one lot for the LORD, and the other lot for the scapegoat. And Aaron shall bring the goat upon which the LORD's lot fell, and offer him for a sin offering. But the goat, on which the lot fell to be the scapegoat, shall be presented alive before the LORD, to make an atonement with him, and to let him go for a scapegoat into the wilderness.

And Aaron shall bring the bullock of the sin offering, which is for himself, and shall make an atonement for himself, and for his house, and shall kill the bullock of the sin offering which is for himself: And he shall take a censer full of burning coals of fire from off the altar before the LORD, and his hands full of sweet incense beaten small, and bring it within the vail: And he shall put the incense upon the fire before the LORD, that the cloud of the incense may cover the mercy seat that is upon the testimony, that he die not: And he shall take of the blood of the bullock, and sprinkle it with his finger upon the mercy seat eastward; and before the mercy seat shall he sprinkle of the blood with his finger seven times.

Then shall he kill the goat of the sin offering, that is for the people, and bring his blood within the vail, and do with that blood as he did with the blood of the bullock, and sprinkle it upon the mercy seat, and before the mercy seat: And he shall make an atonement for the holy place, because of the uncleanness of the children of

THE ATONEMENT

Israel, and because of their transgressions in all their sins: and so shall he do for the tabernacle of the congregation, that remaineth among them in the midst of their uncleanness.

And there shall be no man in the tabernacle of the congregation when he goeth in to make an atonement in the holy place, until he come out, and have made an atonement for himself, and for his household, and for all the congregation of Israel.

And he shall go out unto the altar that is before the LORD, and make an atonement for it; and shall take of the blood of the bullock, and of the blood of the goat, and put it upon the horns of the altar round about. And he shall sprinkle of the blood upon it with his finger seven times, and cleanse it, and hallow it from the uncleanness of the children of Israel.

And when he hath made an end of reconciling the holy place, and the tabernacle of the congregation, and the altar, he shall bring the live goat: And Aaron shall lay both his hands upon the head of the live goat, and confess over him all the iniquities of the children of Israel, and all their transgressions in all their sins, putting them upon the head of the goat, and shall send him away by the hand of a fit man into the wilderness: And the goat shall bear upon him all their iniquities unto a land not inhabited: and he shall let go the goat in the wilderness.

And Aaron shall come into the tabernacle of the congregation, and shall put off the linen garments, which he put on when he went into the holy place, and shall leave them there: And he shall wash his flesh with water in the holy place, and put on his garments, and come forth, and offer his burnt offering, and the burnt offering of the people, and make an atonement for himself, and for the people. And the fat of the sin offering shall he burn upon the altar. And he that let go the goat for the scapegoat shall wash his clothes, and bathe his flesh in water, and afterward come into the camp.

And the bullock for the sin offering, and the goat for the sin offering, whose blood was brought in to make atonement in the holy place, shall one carry forth without the camp; and they shall burn in the fire their skins, and their flesh, and their dung. And he that burneth them shall wash his clothes, and bathe his flesh in water, and afterward he shall come into the camp.

And this shall be a statute for ever unto you: that in the seventh month, on the tenth day of the month, ye shall afflict your souls, and do no work at all, whether it be one of your own country, or a stranger that sojourneth among you: For on that day shall the priest make an atonement for you, to cleanse you, that ye may be clean from all your sins before the LORD. It shall be a sabbath of rest unto you, and ye shall afflict your souls, by a statute for ever.

THE ATONEMENT

And the priest, whom he shall anoint, and whom he shall consecrate to minister in the priest's office in his father's stead, shall make the atonement, and shall put on the linen clothes, even the holy garments: And he shall make an atonement for the holy sanctuary, and he shall make an atonement for the tabernacle of the congregation, and for the altar, and he shall make an atonement for the priests, and for all the people of the congregation. And this shall be an everlasting statute unto you, to make an atonement for the children of Israel for all their sins once a year. And he did as the LORD commanded Moses.

~Leviticus 16:1-34

And the LORD spake unto Moses, saying, Speak unto the children of Israel, and say unto them, Concerning the feasts of the LORD, which ye shall proclaim to be holy convocations, even these are my feasts. Six days shall work be done: but the seventh day is the sabbath of rest, an holy convocation; ye shall do no work therein: it is the sabbath of the LORD in all your dwellings.

These are the feasts of the LORD, even holy convocations, which ye shall proclaim in their seasons. In the fourteenth day of the first month at even is the LORD's passover. And on the fifteenth day of the same month is the feast of unleavened bread unto the LORD: seven days ye must eat unleavened bread. In the first day ye shall have an holy convocation: ye shall do no servile work therein. But ye shall offer an offering made by fire unto the LORD seven days: in the seventh day is an holy con- vocation: ye shall do no servile work therein.

And the LORD spake unto Moses, saying, Speak unto the children of Israel, and say unto them, When ye be come into the land which I give unto you, and shall reap the harvest thereof, then ye shall bring a sheaf of the firstfruits of your harvest unto the priest: And he shall wave the sheaf before the LORD, to be accepted for you: on the morrow after the sabbath the priest shall wave it. And ye shall offer that day when ye wave the sheaf an he lamb without blemish of the first year for a burnt offering unto the LORD. And the meat offering thereof shall be two tenth deals of fine flour mingled with oil, an offering made by fire unto the LORD for a sweet savour: and the drink offering thereof shall be of wine, the fourth part of an hin.

And ye shall eat neither bread, nor parched corn, nor green ears, until the selfsame day that therein: it shall be a statute for ever in all your dwellings throughout your generations in all your dwellings. And ye shall count unto you from the morrow after the sabbath, from the day that ye brought the sheaf of the wave offering; seven sabbaths shall be complete: Even unto the morrow after the seventh sabbath shall ye number fifty days; and ye shall offer a new meat offering unto the LORD. Ye shall bring out of your habitations two wave loaves of two tenth deals: they shall be of fine flour; they shall be baken with leaven; they are the firstfruits unto the LORD.

And ye shall offer with the bread seven lambs without blemish of the first year, and one young bullock, and two rams: they shall be for a burnt offering unto the LORD, with their meat offering, and their drink offerings, even an offering made by fire, of sweet savour unto the LORD. Then ye shall sacrifice one kid of the goats for a sin offering, and two lambs of the first year for a sacrifice of peace offerings. And the priest shall wave them with the bread of the firstfruits for a wave offering before the LORD, with the two lambs: they shall be holy to the LORD for the priest. And ye shall proclaim on the selfsame day, that it may be an holy convocation unto you: ye shall do no servile work therein: it shall be a statute for ever in all your dwellings throughout your generations.

And when ye reap the harvest of your land, thou shalt not make clean riddance of the corners of thy field when thou reapest, neither shalt thou gather any gleaning of thy harvest: thou shalt leave them unto the poor, and to the stranger: I am the LORD your God.

And the LORD spake unto Moses, saying, Speak unto the children of Israel, saying, In the seventh month, in the first day of the month, shall ye have a sabbath, a memorial of blowing of trumpets, an holy convocation. Ye shall do no servile work therein: but ye shall offer an offering made by fire unto the LORD.

And the LORD spake unto Moses, saying, Also on the tenth day of this seventh month there shall be a day of atonement: it shall be an holy convocation unto you; and ye shall afflict your souls, and offer an offering made by fire unto the LORD. And ye shall do no work in that same day: for it is a day of atonement, to make an atonement for you before the LORD your God. For whatsoever soul it be that shall not be afflicted in that same day, he shall be cut off from among his people. And whatsoever soul it be that doeth any work in that same day, the same soul will I destroy from among his people. Ye shall do no manner of work: it shall be a statute for ever throughout your generations in all your dwellings. It shall be unto you a sabbath of rest, and ye shall afflict your souls: in the ninth day of the month at even, from even unto even, shall ye celebrate your sabbath.

And the LORD spake unto Moses, saying, Speak unto the children of Israel, saying, The fifteenth day of this seventh month shall be the feast of tabernacles for seven days unto the LORD. On the first day shall be an holy convocation: ye shall do no servile work therein. Seven days ye shall offer an offering made by fire unto the LORD: on the eighth day shall be an holy convocation unto you; and ye shall offer an offering made by fire unto the LORD: it is a solemn assembly; and ye shall do no servile work therein. These are the feasts of the LORD, which ye shall proclaim to be holy convocations, to offer an offering made by fire unto the LORD, a burnt offering, and a meat offering, a sacrifice, and drink offerings, every thing upon his day: Beside the sabbaths of the LORD, and beside your gifts, and beside all your vows, and beside all your freewill offerings, which ye give unto the LORD.

Also in the fifteenth day of the seventh month, when ye have gathered in the fruit of the land, ye shall keep a feast unto the LORD seven days: on the first day shall be a sabbath, and on the eighth day shall be a sabbath. And ye shall take you on the first day the boughs of goodly trees, branches of palm trees, and the boughs of thick trees, and willows of the brook; and ye shall rejoice before the LORD your God seven days. And ye shall keep it a feast unto the LORD seven days in the year. It shall be a statute for ever in your generations: ye shall celebrate it in the seventh month. Ye shall dwell in booths seven days; all that are Israelites born shall dwell in booths: That your generations may know that I made the children of Israel to dwell in booths, when I brought them out of the land of Egypt: I am the LORD your God. And Moses declared unto the children of Israel the feasts of the LORD.

~ Leviticus 23:1-44

THE ATONEMENT

Observe the month of Abib, and keep the passover unto the LORD thy God: for in the month of Abib the LORD thy God brought thee forth out of Egypt by night. Thou shalt therefore sacrifice the passover unto the LORD thy God, of the flock and the herd, in the place which the LORD shall choose to place his name there.

Thou shalt eat no leavened bread with it; seven days shalt thou eat unleavened bread therewith, even the bread of affliction; for thou camest forth out of the land of Egypt in haste: that thou mayest remember the day when thou camest forth out of the land of Egypt all the days of thy life. And there shall be no leavened bread seen with thee in all thy coast seven days; neither shall there anything of the flesh, which thou sacrificedst the first day at even, remain all night until the morning.

Thou mayest not sacrifice the passover within any of thy gates, which the LORD thy God giveth thee: But at the place which the LORD thy God shall choose to place his name in, there thou shalt sacrifice the passover at even, at the going down of the sun, at the season that thou camest forth out of Egypt. And thou shalt roast and eat it in the place which the LORD thy God shall choose: and thou shalt turn in the morning, and go unto thy tents. Six days thou shalt eat unleavened bread: and on the seventh day shall be a solemn assembly to the LORD thy God: thou shalt do no work therein.

Seven weeks shalt thou number unto thee: begin to number the seven weeks from such time as thou beginnest to put the sickle to the corn. And thou shalt keep the feast of weeks unto the LORD thy God with a tribute of a freewill offering of thine hand, which thou shalt give unto the LORD thy God, according as the LORD thy God hath blessed thee: And thou shalt rejoice before the LORD thy God, thou, and thy son, and thy daughter, and thy manservant, and thy maidservant, and the Levite that is within thy gates, and the stranger, and the fatherless, and the widow, that are among you, in the place which the LORD thy God hath chosen to place his name there.

And thou shalt remember that thou wast a bondman in Egypt: and thou shalt observe and do these statutes. Thou shalt observe the feast of tabernacles seven days, after that thou hast gathered in thy corn and thy wine: And thou shalt rejoice in thy feast, thou, and thy son, and thy daughter, and thy manservant, and thy maidservant, and the Levite, the stranger, and the fatherless, and the widow, that are within thy gates.

Seven days shalt thou keep a solemn feast unto the LORD thy God in the place which the LORD shall choose: because the LORD thy God shall bless thee in all thine increase, and in all the works of thine hands, therefore thou shalt surely rejoice.

Three times in a year shall all thy males appear before the LORD thy God in the place which he shall choose; in the feast of unleavened bread, and in the feast of weeks, and in the feast of tabernacles: and they shall not appear before the LORD empty: Every man shall give as he is able, according to the blessing of the LORD thy God which he hath given thee.

~ Deuteronomy 16:1-17

ABOUT THE AUTHOR

ROD PARSLEY, best-selling author of more than sixty books, is the dynamic pastor of World Harvest Church in Columbus, Ohio, a church with worldwide ministries and a global outreach. As a highly-sought-after crusade and conference speaker whom God has raised up as a prophetic voice to America and the world, Parsley is calling people to Jesus Christ through the good news of the Gospel.

He oversees 13 major ministries, including: Bridge of Hope Missions; Harvest Preparatory School; Valor Christian College; and the *Breakthrough* broadcast, a television and radio show seen by millions and broadcast to nearly 200 countries around the world.

Parsley's refreshingly direct style encourages Christians to examine and eradicate sin from their lives. A fearless champion of living God's way, Parsley follows the high standard set by Jesus Christ and compels his readers to do the same. He and his wife, Joni, have two children, Ashton and Austin.